My Body Belongs to Me

from My Head to My Toes

Created by
pro familia

Illustrated by
Dagmar Geisler

Preface by
**International Center
for Assault Prevention (ICAP)**

Translated by
Connie Stradling Morby

Sky Pony Press
New York

First English Translation © 2014 by Skyhorse Publishing, Inc.

Published by arrangement with Loewe Verlag GmbH.
Title of the original German edition: *Mein Körper gehört mir!*
© 1994, 2002, 2011 Loewe Verlag GmbH, Bindlach
Author: pro familia Darmstadt, Martina Neukirch-Seibert, Gudrun Dittrich, Ursula Hagedorn
Illustrations: Dagmar Geisler

Sky Pony Press books may be purchased in bulk at special discounts for sales promotion, corporate gifts, fund-raising, or educational purposes. Special editions can also be created to specifications. For details, contact the Special Sales Department, Sky Pony Press, 307 West 36th Street, 11th Floor, New York, NY 10018 or info@skyhorsepublishing.com.

Sky Pony® is a registered trademark of Skyhorse Publishing, Inc.®, a Delaware corporation.

Visit our website at www.skyponypress.com.

20 19 18 17 16 15 14 13 12

Manufactured in China, October 2021
This product conforms to CPSIA 2008

Library of Congress Cataloging-in-Publication Data is available on file.

ISBN: 978-1-62636-345-8

Dear Grown-ups,

All children worldwide, regardless of where they are from, are vulnerable to potential exploitation and abuse. Reducing children's vulnerability to victimization needs to start at an early age. However, it does not have to be a formidable task. Parents and caregivers can begin this process by talking to even very young children about their rights to a safe body.

My Body Belongs to Me from My Head to My Toes is a wonderful learning tool that can help facilitate such a discussion. This simple and beautifully illustrated book will help your children to establish a good self-image by being proud of their own body. They will also learn that there are personal body boundaries which they themselves have the right to set. If these limits are violated, it is also their right to be assertive and voice their disapproval. Additionally, this story teaches that if the person violating these boundaries doesn't stop, then the child does not have to keep a secret but is empowered to find a trusted adult to tell.

We would recommend you use this book as a building block to set a foundation of safety, and to create a reduction of vulnerability, as well as increased self-awareness and empowerment that can last your child a lifetime.

—The International Center for Assault Prevention (ICAP), 2013

To learn more about the Child Assault Prevention (CAP) program and the International Center, please visit www.interantionalCAP.org.

I'm Clara and I have something really special: my body! It belongs only to me.

When I was still a baby, my body looked quite different.

But I'm growing and growing. And my body and I are changing.

I'm proud of myself and my body.

Sometimes I want to be
close to somebody. When
I do, our bodies touch.

It feels nice and cozy when Papa hugs me. I like to cuddle with him.

It's comfortable sitting on my granny's lap. We are very close to each other then.

Holding a little baby is not so easy. You have to be close when you hold a baby's hands.

When I tickle my friend,
we touch each other
and laugh a lot.

Touching each other can be something very special. But I alone decide if and by whom I'd like to be touched.

Sometimes I simply don't
want to be touched.

I don't think it's funny when somebody tickles me way too much. I don't want that to happen.

I think it's icky when somebody gives me a big, fat, sloppy kiss. I don't want that type of touch either.

I also don't like it when a dog
licks me with his wet tongue.

I feel trapped when somebody holds me too tight. I don't want to be held like that.

Whenever somebody touches me
and I don't like it . . .

. . . I say, "Stop it. Don't touch me.
I don't want you to."

If I'm asked to touch somebody, but I don't want to, I just don't do it.

I say, "No, I don't want to touch you. I don't feel like it."

You should try saying it too, loud and clear: "Don't touch me! I don't want you to!" You can also say: "I don't want to touch you! I don't feel like it!"

I think it's great that people touch each other when they both want to. Don't you think so too?

But when I don't feel comfortable, then I don't let anyone touch me. I say, "No!" That's because I decide when I would like to be touched and by whom. And you should too.

Sometimes a person doesn't stop when you say, "No!" and keeps on touching in a way that doesn't feel good. You must stick up for yourself. If you can't do it by yourself, then tell somebody you trust about it, and they will help you.

Think about it. Your body belongs only to you.
It's something very special.

Resources for Adults

International Center for Assault Prevention (ICAP)
107 Gilbreth Parkway, Suite 200
Mullica Hill, NJ 08062
Phone: 1-800-258-3189
Email: childassaultpreventon@gmail.com
Website: www.internationalcap.org/

U.S. Department of Health and Human Services
Administration for Children & Families
Child Welfare Information Gateway
Children's Bureau/ACYE
1250 Maryland Avenue, SW
Eighth Floor
Washington, DC 20024
Phone: 1-800-394-3366
Email: info@childwelfare.gov
Website: www.childwelfare.gov

Childhelp USA
(National Child Abuse Hotline)
15757 N. 78th Street, Ste. B
Scottsdale, AZ 85260
Phone (hotline): 1-800-4-A-CHILD (1-800-422-4453)
Website: www.childhelp.org

National Criminal Justice Reference Services (NCJRS)
For resources and publications related to the prevention
of and response to cases of child abuse.
Website: www.ncjrs.gov/childabuse/